My Five Super Senses

I SMELL IT!

Theresa Emminizer

PowerKiDS press

PK Beginners

I use my nose to smell things.

I smell the flowers.
They are sweet!

I smell my shoes.
They are stinky!

I smell the air outside.

I smell cookies.
Yummy!

I smell the berries
in the garden.

I smell garlic.
It smells strong!

I smell the fire.

It's smokey!

I smell the baby.

He needs a change!

I smell the bath.
It smells clean!

There are so many things to smell!

Published in 2024 by The Rosen Publishing Group, Inc.
2544 Clinton Street, Buffalo, NY 14224

First Edition

Editor: Theresa Emminizer
Book Design: Rachel Rising

Photo Credits: Cover, p. 1 Patcharida/Shutterstock.com; p. 3 Krakenimages.com/Shutterstock.com; p. 5 Daria Grebenchuk/Shutterstock.com; p. 7 esthermm/Shutterstock.com; p. 9 KlingSup/Shutterstock.com; p. 11 Cavan-Images/Shutterstock.com; p. 13 Mirshik/Shutterstock.com; p. 15 Purino/Shutterstock.com; p. 17 kurtjurgen/Shutterstock.com; p. 19 Miljan Zivkovic/Shutterstock.com; p. 21 XiXinXing/Shutterstock.com; p. 23 Gelpi/Shutterstock.com.

Library of Congress Cataloging-in-Publication Data
Names: Emminizer, Theresa, author.
Title: I smell it! / Theresa Emminizer.
Description: [Buffalo] : PowerKids Press, [2023] | Series: My five super senses | Audience: Grades K-1
Identifiers: LCCN 2023027829 (print) | LCCN 2023027830 (ebook) | ISBN 9781499443387 (library binding) | ISBN 9781499443370 (paperback) | ISBN 9781499443394 (ebook)
Subjects: LCSH: Smell–Juvenile literature. | Nose–Juvenile literature.
Classification: LCC QP458 .E46 2023 (print) | LCC QP458 (ebook) | DDC 612.8/6–dc23/eng/20230614
LC record available at https://lccn.loc.gov/2023027829
LC ebook record available at https://lccn.loc.gov/2023027830

Manufactured in the United States of America

CPSIA Compliance Information: Batch #CWPK24. For further information contact Rosen Publishing at 1-800-237-9932.

Find us on